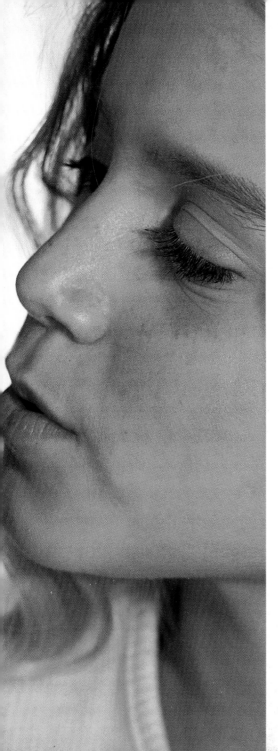

Imma...

Budgerigars

Everything about
Purchase, Care,
Nutrition, Behavior,
and Training

Photography: Uwe Anders and
other animal photographers

Illustrations: György Jankovics

Translated and Adapted by
Matthew M. Vriends, Ph.D.

BARRON'S

2 CONTENTS

TYPICAL
BUDGERIGARS

- **Have colorful plumage**
- **Are inquisitive and cheerful**
- **Are loyal to their human friends**
- **Love companionship**
- **Are chatterboxes to partners and humans**
- **Are always tolerant as a group**
- **Learn to talk**
- **Are always loving mothers**

Budgerigars (budgies), often called parakeets, enjoy fun and games. They love to exercise and swing, will fly curiously all over the place, and perch with confidence on their owner's head or shoulder when carried around in the living room or den. When they are carried, they often nibble on little salt particles on the skin of their human escort.

You and your feathered friend will have the most fun, however, inventing new games. The bird will solve simple arithmetic problems, play water polo with grapes, and make music with ornaments, glass marbles, and little bells.

THINK BEFORE YOU BUY

1 Budgies need a roomy cage in which to fly comfortably; this type of cage can be expensive.

2 Budgies like people, but their social utterances may be disturbing. You have to settle for that.

3 Budgies need free-flying sessions daily. There may be some droppings, and sometimes budgies nibble on furniture and houseplants— so be tolerant.

4 Properly cared for, budgies can live to be a healthy 15 to 20 years old. They dislike change of ownership, however, so you are fully responsible for your budgie's well-being.

5 Care and management are simple, but quality time and some expense are involved.

6 Budgies are not your everyday pet, like a cat or dog.

7 Daily "get-togethers" are essential if you want to gain your budgie's trust.

8 Before you buy a budgie, be sure you will be able to take care of your pet if it should become ill.

9 If you have other pets, make sure that they will accept your budgie (see page 29).

10 Before you buy a bird, consult your physician if you think you or members of your family are allergic to feathers or feather dust.

One Bird or a Pair?

Budgies are by nature gregarious birds. In their native Australia they live in large flocks, so they will be much happier in your home when kept in twos or more. A singleton will only be happy if it can develop a strong bond with a human who then automatically serves as a surrogate partner, but even a single budgie will miss its natural partner; therefore, it is recommended that you keep a pair.

Male or Female?

A male and female budgie in love is the very best situation; you don't have to worry about offspring—as long as you don't give them a nest box.

✔ If you like to study budgies, buy a pair. Male and female (hen) will be most cheerful and entertaining and you will soon discover that a pair offers the most excitement.

✔ Even two males may like each other but this is obviously not as exciting as a true pair because many behavior traits will remain dormant when you have two males.

✔ Never ever keep two hens together as they will constantly fight—with often bloody results.

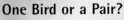

PURCHASE AND HOUSING

The budgie is one of the most popular pet birds in America, if not in the world. It is easy to keep, easy to tame, and very easy to love. From the original grass-green wild bird, the budgerigar (or "good bird"), breeders have developed a rainbow of spectacular colors and markings.

The Little Australian Parrot

We are flying in a small airplane over a fascinating, rather arid region in Central Australia. Under us lies a flat open landscape, dotted with eucalyptus trees and bushes, with ancient, craggy rock hills and creeks. In this habitat budgies live a migratory life; as rivers and ponds tend to dry out, they are forced to move away in order to find water. Meanwhile, the temperature is rising quickly; it's 11:00 A.M., and already 113°F (45°C); we have not seen any rain for weeks. Budgies use trees to hide in and to nest in, and the grasslands are the source of their meals. We can see them move by the hundreds from their nesting places to the grasslands, a veritable cloud of glimmering green birds moving on quickly beating wings and decoratively spread tails.

Life in a Flock

Wild budgies are primarily green- and yellow-colored birds—little powerhouses that are always on the move. It is a fascinating sight

Budgies love to find food between the branches of their bird tree.

to observe their comings and goings at a water source where they quench their thirst in only a few seconds. In dry years, thousands of budgies may gather around one watering place, no matter how shallow it is.

After drinking, the birds fly to nearby eucalyptus trees to rest. Because of their coloring they are hardly visible between the leaves. The flock usually drinks between the morning feeding and the midday siesta, and again in the late afternoon. This daily rhythm is not always predictable, however—a lot depends on the temperature.

Wild budgies sleep in different places every night (in contrast to pet birds which keep the same sleeping place for years). Sleeping as a flock guarantees protection against predators. If the flock is disturbed, all birds fly up together and look for another tree on which to settle down. Our pet birds, too, stick together to a certain daily behavior; a single bird, however, will never undertake any action by itself.

Adjusting to the Environment

The budgie's way of life and all its behavior patterns are geared to survival in its "hostile" surroundings; for example, male budgies are

sexually precocious. By the time they are three to four months old, their testes are functional and they have their adult plumage.

During long periods of drought, the birds often have to fly several hundred miles before they find an area that offers enough food and water. During extensive dry periods, thousands may die and the survivors move on to areas with more clement conditions. A farmer in Central Australia once fished five tons of dead birds from one of his cattle water stations! For the birds that are exhausted by long flights and weakened by lack of water, these stations are veritable death traps.

The only way the budgie species can survive is to compensate by reproducing quickly and in

A flock of wild budgies drinking and bathing at a water hole.

great numbers when conditions in their habitat are favorable. After the reproductive cycle, the native birds do not mate until the onset of a new season is announced by external factors, such as the length of the days, and then the cycle starts all over again.

✔ Budgies are sexually precocious and will start searching for a partner when only a few months old. They mate for life (they are monogamous). Budgies in the wild react quickly to rainfall, and within a few days will begin to copulate and raise a family; two or three broods per pair are very possible.

✔ The wild budgie incubates her four to eight eggs in suitable holes in trees, hollows, stumps, fence posts, and the like, without using any nesting materials. Insects (ants, for example) and especially their larvae keep the nest cavity clean.

✔ There is no territorial defense. Budgies live in flocks or colonies and communal nesting is common. Various nests can be found in the same tree or on the same branch of a tree.

From Wild Budgie to Pet Bird

Their exceptional adaptability and talent to be able to make the best out of every situation is undoubtedly the reason that budgies became the most beloved pet birds in the world.

For more than 100 years they have given us many color mutations and their size has increased substantially since John Gould introduced the first live budgies into England in 1840. A bird merchant sold the first pair for a paltry 27 British pounds, which today would come to more than $1,000. Budgies are supposed to have reached the European continent about ten years later, and became instantly popular.

Sensing an opportunity to make money, sailors caught budgerigars by the thousands and brought them to Europe. The few birds that survived the arduous voyage did not live very long because no one knew how to feed and care for these exotic pets. However, one hardy female budgie flew into an aviary and laid her eggs in a hollowed-out coconut. Her brood was the first to be successfully reared in captivity.

By the turn of the century, budgies were being bred by the hundreds of thousands. People quickly discovered that budgies were easy to breed and Australia's ban of 1894, prohibiting the catching and trading of wild parakeets, was hardly felt. It comes as no surprise that, in view of the quantities, mutations soon began to surface (see page 12).

The fact that our colorful pet budgies still resemble their native counterparts is in itself an astonishing fact (see page 9). Evidently, aviculturists only "changed" the birds' exterior; in their behavior they remain Aussies; therefore we have to understand their behavior and genetic structure.

The dead branch presents an ideal breeding cavity.

BUDGERIGAR
PORTRAITS

The scientific name of the wild budgie, *Melopsittacus undulatus*, indicates the wavy line pattern of the feathers. Pet parakeets, however, come in various colors and with different markings.

Yellow face white mauve (left); recessive pied gray (right)

The albino is pure white.

Normal gray green male

Normal violet (left); cinnamon sky blue (right)

Light green (left); white blue (right)

Recessive pied gray (left); dark green (right)

Opaline dark blue (left); gray (right)

Pied dark green (top); Isabel green (left); Australian dominant pied gray green (right)

Green or blue—in the morning they all clean, stretch, and scratch.

Description of Budgies

Wild parakeets are somewhat smaller and lighter than their domesticated counterparts, measuring 6¼ to 8 inches (16–20 cm) from beak to tip of tail. The wild birds are not as colorful as our pets at home; they are mostly green and yellow with brown to black stripes on the wings and back. Yellow and blue parakeets are occasionally seen in the wild, but they probably do not live long because their conspicuous coloring makes them an easy target for predators. The head is yellow with narrow black stripes, the face (or mask) pale yellow from beak to throat. On the sides, the mask is marked off by longish, violet "sideburns" (see photo page 11), below which are three black spots running in a line toward the center of the throat. The tail is very long. There are many color mutations (see page 12). Domesticated birds are somewhat larger in size, and heavier.

Buying Budgies

Always buy first-rate stock—that's the most important rule. If you expect pleasure and favorable breeding results from your hobby, you have to decide that only the very best is good enough; therefore, take your time to observe the birds offered for sale.

✔ Birds that are quiet and act frightened are difficult to tame. Look only for active and playful ones.

✔ Watch the bird that moves quickly, grooms itself frequently, has active contact with its companions, and eats and drinks at short intervals. Chances are that you are looking at a healthy little fellow.

✔ Birds that affectionately touch each other or are rubbing their beaks together could be your first ideal couple.

✔ Looking for a pet? Buy a five- to six-month-old budgie. Young birds are easy to recognize—they have big, black button eyes (the white iris is still invisible) and a wavy barring over the entire head.

Company Is Important

Keep parakeets in pairs (see page 7). A budgie pet bird will be happy only if it can develop a strong bond to a human. It doesn't matter if you have two birds of the same sex because one of them will in time assume the role of the missing gender; however, keeping two females together is not recommended.

A full-grown (adult) male budgie usually has bright blue ceres (depending on the mutation), while a female has beige or brownish ones. The throat spots in young birds are smaller and more oblong than round as in adults.

Young birds also have a much darker beak than fully grown budgies. In Harlequins the ceres stay light beige into adulthood in both sexes.

Tip: Females have fine, hardly visible, light to whitish rings around the nostrils.

Checklist
Tips for Buying a Bird

1 The bird should be active and interact with other budgies.

2 Its plumage should hug the body smoothly and have a muted sheen.

3 Tail and wing feathers must be fully formed and should never be bent and stick out at an angle.

4 The feathers around the vent should be clean, not soiled from diarrhea.

5 Feet and toes should be straight and clean; the first and fourth are pointing forward, the second and third backward (zygodactyl).

6 Never buy an obese bird; it will always be listless, and susceptible to various diseases.

Before You Make a Deal

Don't act on impulse. Look around with a critical eye in various pet shops and breeding facilities. Pay attention to the following points:

✔ Ask about the background of the birds. Where are they from? Were they kept in clean cages that were large enough?

✔ Did they have sufficient food and fresh drinking water?

✔ Is there clean gravel or other appropriate bedding on the bottom of the cage? (No newspaper!)

✔ Are the birds related? (Generally, inbreeding should be avoided.)

The Band (Ring)

When you buy a budgie, it is often wearing a band (called a "ring" in England) on its leg that guarantees that it comes from a breeder who belongs to a recognized bird society. You should check the banded leg frequently because the bands give rise to many problems. If the band gets caught on something, for instance, the bird will try to yank its leg free and may injure itself. If the leg then swells up,

the band hinders the blood flow, in which case the band should be removed by an experienced breeder or avian veterinarian (see page 59).

Important Points

When you buy a cage, keep in mind that your parakeet's future home should in no way be a prison, but a refuge where it can eat and sleep in safety. Select a quiet, light location in the living room or den.

The Bird Cage

Cages come in many designs and various sizes, but remember: Cages should have greater length than height, since the natural flight pattern of a bird is horizontal, not vertical.

✔ A budgie cage should measure at least 20 inches long × 12 inches wide × 18 inches high (50 cm × 30 cm × 45 cm); ideal dimensions are 40 inches × 20 inches × 32 inches (100 cm × 50 cm × 80 cm). Regardless of size, your active bird will still need several hours of free flying a day; otherwise, it will become listless and will die before its time.

✔ Rectangular cages with a large front and back are preferable. Round or pagoda-like cages with gables and turrets are inappropriate, as they hamper the bird in its freedom of movement.

✔ The bars of at least two side walls (preferably front and back) should run horizontally so the bird will be able to climb with feet and beak—its third "leg."

✔ The bars should be chromeplated or made of brass. Cages made of softwood or plastic will soon succumb to the budgie's active beak.

This water bowl can be used for a bath, but don't fill it to the rim.

✔ The cage door should be attached like a gangplank so the bird can easily land on it in order to get inside.
✔ The bottom pan should be made of plastic.
✔ The sand drawer should easily slide in and out.

Furnishing the Cage

Bird sand: It is essential to have clean bird sand for the drawer at all times. This not only serves a sanitary function but also contributes to the bird's health.

Perches: They should be made of wood and be of different thicknesses (½ and ¾ inch [12 mm and 20 mm]). The bird's toes should not reach all the way around the perch.
✔ Budgies love to gnaw on anything—including their perches. Replace them when

In order to get food, the budgie will set all toys in motion.

necessary. Hang a cuttlebone in the cage for your bird to sharpen its beak on. You can find these in your pet supply store.
✔ Put fresh twigs from willow, elder, and apple trees into the cage for the birds to nibble on. The change from quite thin to very thick natural branches offers the muscles of the bird's feet the required exercise and keeps the nails short.
✔ Don't use branches that have been exposed to automobile exhausts or that have been sprayed with insecticide.
✔ Install perches in such a way that the birds can't foul each other.

Food cups: There should be two—one for daily seeds or pellets, the other for fresh water. They should have plastic shields to protect them from droppings from above. The use of water bottles is preferred. Various semioval dishes that can be hung on bars or placed on the floor are also available. Many budgies quickly learn to use these new utensils, but others have a hard time dealing with them; therefore, it's important to leave the familiar dishes in the cage when other dispensers are first introduced until the birds have become accustomed to them.

A bathhouse: This is essential. The best kind is one that can be hung in the door opening. The bathhouse's floor should be grooved so that the bird will not slip while bathing (see page 52).

Toys: Budgies like all kind of toys, as long as they are safe. They provide some distraction and—most important—lots of fun. They will help them avoid boredom and stress.

✔ Small branches of willow, oak, alder, poplar, mountain ash, or fruit tree branches are greatly appreciated. Alternate them.

✔ Budgies like swings of all sorts, solid plastic balls, ladders, whiffle balls with or without a bell inside, or plastic birds that can be clamped to a perch.

✔ Mirrors are also very popular, although singleton males often become stressed and nervous by seeing their reflection, which they regard as a possible partner or, more often, as a rival.

The Climbing Tree

Reserve approximately a square yard of your living room or den for the budgie and set up a climbing tree. Use as large and heavy a bucket as you can (approximately 3 feet [91 cm] in diameter), and fill it with potting soil. Plant

After a great deal of flying around the room, it is good to rest and play on a delicious handmade swing.

three to four long, sturdy, natural branches or bamboo sticks vertically in the bucket and connect them at two or three levels with horizontal branches of varying thicknesses and shapes. To tie the branches together, you can use natural fiber strips, the ends of which have been thinly covered with a nontoxic glue for long wear. Place some potted vines in the bucket between the vertical branches. Cover the potting soil with a layer of bird gravel, so that the droppings can easily be removed with a slotted spoon.

The Aviary

When you have more than four budgies, an aviary is in order as the large cages described above are too stressful for two pairs of birds. Note the following:

✔ It is very difficult to tame many birds instead of only two, as they will display more interest in each other than in the hobbyist.

✔ They produce more droppings and require much more care.

✔ An aviary takes up quite a lot of space, as the birds need room to fly. Obviously they don't have to fly free in the room anymore; therefore, an aviary should be at least 8 feet long, 5 feet high, and 3 feet wide (2.5 m × 1.5 m × 1 m).

There are various models available in pet supply stores, or you can construct one yourself. Be creative!

Indoor aviary: This type of aviary is not recommended as it is impossible to place the birds outside (for a shower). Proper ventilation often presents problems too, as, due to their high metabolism, budgies need a great deal of oxygen.

A combined indoor-outdoor aviary: This type is ideal as there is access from the inside to the outside aviary via a window or such.

Outside or garden aviary: This is the most ideal housing but is only effective if there is a night shelter that can be heated; birds become sluggish very quickly in cold surroundings (see also page 16).

The Right Place for the Cage

A budgie's cage is its refuge, the place where it feels safe.

✔ The cage should have a permanent location where other pets (cats, dogs) can't bother the birds, such as the living room or den.

✔ The location of the cage should be absolutely free from drafts.

TIP

The 15-Minute Rain

Wild budgies live in arid habitats and become very active when the rains start, so let your birds enjoy a light shower regularly; take out food cups and cuttlebone, and place the cage in the rain for about 15 minutes. The birds will expose their entire body to the raindrops, but if they act frightened, put them inside and try again another time, a few minutes at a time. Don't give up—remember, it takes budgies a while to get used to new experiences.

✔ The bars of the cage should be horizontal, not vertical, because budgies like to climb. The space between bars should measure about $\frac{1}{2}$ inch (12 mm) so the bird can't squeeze through.

✔ Birds are happiest when they can watch humans from above. There should be nothing above the cage because budgies become frightened by activities over their heads.

✔ Don't place the cage directly in front of a window; it is too cold in the winter and too hot in the summer. Place the cage in a corner or on a wide, sturdy shelf that is attached securely to the wall.

Inappropriate Locations

✔ The kitchen: Too many dangers, such as harmful vapors, hot burners, pots and pans with liquid or hot contents, cleaners, and other chemicals that are toxic for the bird (and humans). Also, it can be too drafty when the kitchen has to be aired.

✔ A child's room: Life here is too boring because children spend most of the day in school, engaging in sports, and so on. The living room or den remains the best location.
✔ Never move the cage around.

Bringing Your Budgie Home

The bird should be placed in a small cardboard box, equipped with a few air holes. This box is usually supplied by the pet store or breeder. Carry the box in your hand and keep it from being jostled. Protect it from the cold by loosely wrapping your coat around it. Get your bird home as quickly as possible. Everything there should be ready and set up for the first 24 hours. Once home, open the box on one side and hold it in front of the open cage door, but without leaving any cracks for escape. If the

The bird tree with natural branches can become a beloved mini-environment for any budgie.

bird hesitates to move into its new home, start tilting the box until the bird begins to slide and finally lands in the cage. Close the cage door as soon as the bird is inside and move away. Leave the bird alone for the next few hours. Provided with drink, food, and a spray of millet clamped to one of the bars, the newcomer can look around at its surroundings without any people to distract and frighten it. Try to avoid anything during the first few weeks that might put your budgie into a state of discomfort or panic:
✔ Don't slam doors or make abrupt movements; don't scream or quarrel nearby.

✔ Avoid glaring evening lights; only soft light should reach the cage.

✔ Avoid direct exposure to a television screen, loud music, and so on. The shooting in television police and murder mystery shows is especially frightening to birds.

The Great Escape

About six of ten budgies kept as house pets fly away and are never recovered. They become lost because their surroundings are unfamiliar to them, and they are unable to orient themselves to find the way home. In their Australian natural habitat, wild budgerigars have had no need to develop homing instincts, because the flock, moving as one, alights in a different location each evening to spend the night in the shelter of trees. If a tame budgie doesn't fly into a welcoming window and settle in with a new family, it will perish in a hostile climate or fall victim to dogs, cats, or raptors (birds of prey).

Open doors and windows tempt the naturally curious bird to explore a new environment. Never leave a window open unless your bird's exit is blocked by a solid screen, and repair any holes, however small, in screens throughout your house. The tiniest rip in a screen easily can be enlarged by an adventuresome budgie's beak, and before you know it, your bird has slipped out of the house.

When you let your budgie out of the cage so you can clean it, or when the bird is free to fly around the room, make sure to alert other family members to keep windows and doors closed. (See Parakeets, Masters of Flight, page 25.)

If a budgie loses a large feather, a new one will grow back within a few weeks.

The First Few Hours in a Cage

After arriving home, give your budgie enough time to examine its cage and surroundings. The next day, however, approach the cage quietly, offer fresh water and food, and start talking to your new friend for 15 to 30 minutes. Repeat the bird's chosen name often. Soon it will react to its new name. If it starts eating a few seeds or picks at some millet spray, this can be considered a sign that the worst is over.

The First Few Days and Weeks

Try to avoid anything that might put your budgie into a state of discomfort or panic, such as:

✔ Slamming doors
✔ Loud talking and screaming
✔ Abrupt movements
✔ Glaring lights during evening hours
✔ Appearing suddenly before your bird's cage with a startling hat, and such.

Speak to your budgie soothingly, and say its name whenever you come into the room. Try to do the feeding and routine cleaning chores at the same time every day (see page 35). Once the bird pecks at its food, has a sip of water, and starts moving around, you can tell it has begun to feel at home.

Hand-taming a Budgie

Start taming your bird as soon as possible.

Phase 1: Offer seed from your hand inside the cage every day at the same time. At first the bird will probably not dare to get close enough

Speak softly and offer millet seed.

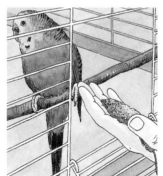

Repeat your bird's name in a soft voice.

It's difficult for a bird to resist a millet spray.

Never grab a bird except in a great emergency, and never try to catch it in flight. Such experiences could destroy the bird's trust that you have worked patiently to develop. Hold your finger in the air and wait for the budgie to alight on it.

to your hand to peck at millet but will only eye it briefly and then look away. Remain motionless and talk softly (at eye level) to the bird.

Phase 2: Once your budgie shows little or no fear of your hand, you can stretch out

Bringing Tame Birds Together

1. Place cages close together.

2. When the birds start to interact, open both cage doors. Let them fly free in the room (see page 25).

3. Parakeets understand each other almost immediately. After their flight they will be tired and cuddle together relaxed and peacefully. If they are fearful, do the same as above but wait a day before opening the cage doors.

Parakeets getting acquainted through the bars of their cages.

your forefinger and gently stroke the bird's breast and lower abdomen, gradually working your finger toward its feet. By gently pressing the budgie's lower abdomen, you can induce the bird to transfer itself to your finger.

Phase 3: Once the budgie is on your finger, gently withdraw your hand through the cage door, all the time softly talking to the bird. The first time out of its cage, the bird will want to

fly around (see page 25), but will soon return to its familiar cage. Use a fixed command, such as *"Come"* to have it return to the cage.

Phase 4: After the bird has become accustomed to the room and is able to return to its cage on command, allow it to transfer from one hand to the other by jumping or stepping, as much as it wants—a very pleasant and relaxing activity for both you and your bird. Two birds should be trained in different rooms and brought together when both are familiar with phase 4.

You should always be patient and consistent when training budgies to get along with each other. If at first they fight or are frightened, take them to their separate rooms and go back to Phase 3 until you think the birds are ready to go on to Phase 4 and perhaps become reacquainted.

It is great fun for your budgie to sit on your shoulder and nibble at your hair.

In their native habitat, Australia, budgerigars like to or have to travel and are indeed flying acrobats. If you give the birds the opportunity to fly free in a room, it will benefit their health.

A Requirement: Free Flight

To deprive birds of free flying is cruel. Free flight is necessary for the bird's health. It has a positive influence on the muscular system, heart, and blood circulation. The bones of a bird are hollow, greatly reducing its body weight and contributing to flight efficiency. Feathers, also, are very light and are formed by the skin. They help maintain a constant body temperature and act as a water repellent.

Parakeets, Masters of Flight

Budgerigars fly long and fast, often traveling more than 70 miles (113 km) an hour as they roam across the plains and semideserts of their native continent in search of food and water. They are able to change direction fast and efficiently, like swallows.

One morning your budgie will show its pleasure at seeing you and shake its plumage vigorously. This behavior indicates that your bird would very much like to explore a wider

Birds love to just sit in a basket that is filled with herbs and nibble now and then on these healthy greens.

territory; therefore, satisfy its desire and let it fly free in the room.

A Bird-Proof Room

With a weight of only about 1.4 ounces (39.6 g), parakeets are rather defenseless creatures—and there are many dangers lurking about. These small, agile avian wonders can discover fascinating things to which humans are quite oblivious. The room, therefore, must be kept bird-safe. To make sure your bird won't encounter any mishaps (see page 27) and can enjoy free flying, even without constant supervision, a few useful procedures are recommended:

✔ Budgies may attack furniture, wallpaper, posters, books, and papers with a passion, decorating them with innumerable chew marks.

✔ Female budgies like to keep themselves busy with their beaks and can cause extensive damage to any material they find fit to chew.

✔ The bird should never be in contact with poisonous indoor plants; it will chew them if given the chance just to satisfy its curiosity.

✔ Be especially careful with cacti of all kinds and other plants with thorny or prickly parts, as the birds can hurt their eyes on them.

The First Flight in the Room

If at first your budgie just sits on its perch, staring through the open cage door as though hypnotized, and doesn't immediately launch itself into the free air, don't worry. Remember that it has probably never before had a chance to fly, as, in the nest box there wasn't enough room, and in the communal cage the bird probably couldn't do much more than flutter its winds.

Give the budgie plenty of time: At some point it won't be able to resist the temptation to take a closer look at the room it sees beyond the open rectangle of its cage. Perhaps it will first climb on top of the cage but soon the urge to fly will overcome fear and your budgie will take to its wings and cross the room for the first time.

Landing maneuvers: Flying itself presents no problems, but landing may be a different story, first of all because your bird probably has never done it before, and secondly because there are so many unfamiliar, frightening objects in the room. With some luck, the bird may be able to land on the cage. If that is the case, leave it up to your budgie whether it wants to have another go at it or whether it prefers to retreat to the safety of the cage. The next day it will probably go about flying with much less hesitation.

How to lure the bird back into the cage: If your budgie lands on the floor, put down some bird seed for it. Budgies love to forage for food on the ground. Then, when you place the cage near the bird a little later, the bird will probably be happy to climb back in. Should the bird land on a bookcase, a lamp, or a curtain rod, talk to it soothingly, and try to lure it back to the cage with a spray of millet. Never lose your patience! This would destroy all the trust in you the bird has developed.

Budgies and Children

Most children love pets; budgies especially get their attention. They are amused by the birds' movements, they love the bright colors of the feathers, and they are fascinated if the bird can talk. They notice the smallest details, and constantly ask questions. They will spend hours watching the interesting behavior of a budgie

If there is a bird tree in the room the bird will land on it safely.

Dangers for Your Budgie

Location	Danger	How to Avoid the Danger
Bathroom	Escape through a window; drowning in the toilet.	Keep the bathroom door closed; allow the bird in only when you are also there.
Bookshelves	Bird hides behind the books and can't get out again without help.	Push books flush against the wall or lay some books flat at intervals.
Floor	If the bird plays on the floor it can be stepped on and killed.	Get in the habit of being extremely careful wherever you step.
Water containers	The bird slips into a bucket, bowl, large glass, or vase, and drowns (soapsuds are often mistaken by the bird for a solid landing site).	Cover containers; don't let the bird fly free when you clean house.
Closets, open drawers	The bird is locked in inadvertently and suffocates or starves to death.	Never leave them open, even a crack.
Poisons	Fatal poisoning can be caused by alcohol, the graphite in pencils, the points of magic markers and ballpoint pens, strong spices, verdigris, adhesives, varnishes, glues, solvents, fertilizers, plastic wrap, cleaners, strong-smelling sprays, laundry detergents, heavy cigarette smoke, smoke from burning teflon-coated pans.	Keep these substances and objects locked away where the bird can't get at them; remove all traces of them.
Stovetop burners	Fatal burns can result if the bird lands on a hot burner or in a pot filled with hot contents.	Put pots or kettles filled with cold water on burners that are still hot; never let the bird fly unsupervised in the kitchen.
Burning candles	Fatal burns can result if the bird flies through the flame.	Do not have candles burning in the room while the bird is flying free.
Wastepaper basket and vases	The bird can slide in, starve to death, or die of heart failure if it feels trapped.	Use woven baskets or line the inside of them with wire mesh; fill vases with sand.

*In the evening, houseplants inspire
adventurous games.*

in or out of its cage, and will get even more
enjoyment from their pet if they are guided
and encouraged by experienced adults.

Learning Responsibility

Many children already have a pet budgie or
want one, but parents must be aware that the
responsibility for the well-being of the pet
cannot be left entirely to the child. With
parental guidance, most children will soon
understand that an animal needs daily care and
regular playtime.

It is important for children to be around
animals while they are growing up in order to
learn love for animals and responsibility for
another creature.

Are Budgies Right for Children?

Don't get a budgie (or any other pet) just for
the child; it should be a family bird for whose
well-being all members of the household feel
responsible. Which animal is suitable?

✔ Children less than eight years old want an
animal primarily to hug and pet and perhaps
are pleading for a dog. Don't get a budgie as a
gesture of compromise. Even the tamest budgie
that likes to have its head scratched cannot
possibly satisfy a child's need for physical
contact with an animal. A young child might

squeeze the bird affectionately and unintentionally cause its death.

✔ For children older than eight years, the budgie is the ideal pet. Children in this age group start dealing with new abilities. They like to make observations and ask many questions. An animal will be treated with more care, and children at that age will concentrate on the animal's needs.

Becoming Friends

Both child and budgie have to learn how to react to each other; then, after a short time, a close friendship results. You can assist them in achieving this goal by:

✔ Hand-taming the bird (see page 22): The child should observe you closely. Place some food in the child's open hand and lead it to the bird. Avoid all sudden movements; don't startle the bird.

✔ Sometimes children seem somewhat rough toward animals. They don't do this intentionally, but because they don't know better. Teach the child that an animal also feels pain.

✔ When a child is allowed to take care of a budgie, it should be made clear that there are many responsibilities attached to the job: hygiene, for example, is very important. A child has to understand that taking care of an animal means investing a lot of time and money in this pet. A pet bird will not be satisfied with the child's needs but only with what it requires in order to live and be happy.

Budgies and Other Domestic Animals

Budgies behave very well with other domestic animals (see photo, page 3). It is practically impossible, however, to get a cat

and a bird to coexist in peace, even though there are reports that suggest that in exceptional cases some animals learn to overcome their natural instincts.

The Right Food

The diet of wild budgerigars includes the seeds of 21 species of plants—a remarkable variety. Most of these plants are grasses. The birds are very quiet when feeding.

Prepared Food

Several excellent commercially prepared foods for birds are on the market. The best-known simple diet consists of a good seed mixture, dried greens and fruits, soft food (egg food), and commercial pellets. These diets work well in practice, and you can feel confident using them for your birds.

These two simply can't get enough of each other!

You must be careful to use seeds that are fresh. Check if they sprout—take a sample of about 100 seeds and place them on a wet paper towel on a plate. Put the plate in a light spot at room temperature. If after four to six days, more than 60 seeds have sprouted, you know all is well.

Seed as the Basic Staple

Our knowledge of the feeding habits of wild parakeets has made it possible to come up with properly balanced seed mixtures that can serve as the basic staple in our pet parakeets' diet. A good seed mix consists of canary grass seed, several millet varieties, oats, niger seed, linseed, thistle, and pellets or crumbles (containing vitamins and minerals). Some mixes have iodine grains to prevent enlargement of the thyroid.

Important Supplements

Raw vegetables: Eggplant, endive, green peas, young dandelion, corn kernels, fresh milky corn, Swiss chard, carrots, and fresh fruits (see Feeding, page 33).

Vitamins: These are crucial to the bird's health. A vitamin supplement is recommended, since it is impossible to check the vitamin content of seeds, fruits, and vegetables.

Minerals and trace elements: These are needed only in minute quantities. Calcium and phosphorus are present in the mineral block the bird uses to sharpen its beak on. Cuttlebone is also used for this purpose, but it should not be given to females about to breed as they sometimes develop egg binding after gnawing on cuttlebone shells.

Grit: Birds need grit to aid the digestive process. It can be purchased from your local pet store.

Snacks: These come in various forms. Honey and fruit sticks are excellent, or seeds glued to

Food tastes twice as good when it can be found on a climbing tree.

heart and bell shapes with sugar syrup and honey. These treats should be offered only once or twice a week to avoid obesity.

Drinking Water

Of course your budgie needs fresh water every day. It needs the liquid to aid in digesting its solid food. Tap water that is not too cold is fine, but if you want to offer your birds something especially healthy, buy noncarbonated mineral water. The label on the bottle usually lists the health-promoting minerals contained in the water. Only sick birds should get boiled water or, if an avian veterinarian recommends it, weak black tea or chamomile tea.

If the drinking water is supplied in a bowl, check several times daily to be sure that the water has not been fouled with droppings, feathers, or seed hulls and, if necessary, replace it.

The water in drinking bottles remains clean. You can hang the bottle on the bars of the cage, and your budgie will quickly learn to drink from it.

TIP

Food and Fun

Always try to trigger the birds' inquisitiveness and their eagerness to explore. In the home, budgies should be kept busy. For this purpose, use open food dishes that you hide somewhere in the room. This game will prevent stress and boredom. These are some tips:

1. Offer only a small amount of greens for a few days, but hide two or three bottles that contain greens and weeds in the room.

2. Place a few dishes filled with seed at eye level outside the cage and release the birds (see page 25). In no time at all, one of the birds will discover the food.

3. After three or four attempts, the birds will quickly realize that they have to be on the lookout for food. Now you can hide the food dishes and the bottles with the greens.

4. You will soon notice how much your birds enjoy this game but be sure that all the birds find their food.

All these little games will help you and your bird bond.

HOW-TO: FEEDING

Budgies are relatively easy to feed; offer them a quality commercial parakeet seed mix. They also enjoy fruits and greens. Budgies like to take a bath in wet, leafy greens—an amusing sight!

Daily Diet

The right seeds should be available at all times in a proper food cup. Fill a cup at least once a day; remove all empty hulls twice a day. All birds have an active metabolism and therefore need small amounts of food several times a day. Never leave a budgie without food for any length of time.

Serve Properly

Fruits and vegetables: Everything should be thoroughly washed, rubbed dry, and peeled, before being offered to the bird.

Greens: Wash greens in lukewarm water. Don't ever offer wilted or rotting greens. ✔ Give greens in the morning. Take all fruits, vegetables, and greens out of the cage in the evening in order to prevent diarrhea and similar disorders.

A budgie needs fresh tap water every day.

Cuttlebone is essential, as are mineral blocks.

The right seed mix is very important.

When you offer your budgie the right food, it will gladly take it from your hand.

Outline

Feeding Plan

On a Daily Basis

Fresh Commercial Seed Mix and Fresh Water (noncarbonated mineral water is ideal)

Greens according to the season	The whole dandelion, chickweed, milk thistle, shepherd's purse, watercress, parsley
Branches with buds	Willow, eucalyptus, lime, poplar, birch, elder
Vegetables according to the season	Broccoli, carrots, alfalfa, dock, celery, sweet potato
Fruits according to the season	Fresh pineapple, apple, apricot, banana, pear, various berries, fresh figs, dates, kiwi
Treats after fun and games	Millet spray, seed sticks, toys, bells

Offer treats only every other day, not daily.

Don't put honey and sweets on their menu too often.

✔ Fresh herbs and wild plants can be found in meadows and fields (unfertilized) or along the roadside (but not too close to the road, because they can become polluted with fumes from traffic). Collect half-ripe and ripe grasses, open weed seedheads, chickweed, watercress, and shepherd's purse.

Roots: All birds love and need the leaves, stems, and especially the roots of dandelions. Watch how the birds go for the minerals.

Caution!
Poisonous plants: Autumn crocus, azalea, balsam pear, boxwood, caladium, castor bean, daffodil, *Dieffenbachia*, avocado, and nightshade varieties. Ask your veterinarian for a complete list of poisonous plants in and around the house.

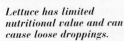

Lettuce has limited nutritional value and can cause loose droppings.

Care and Management

How often . . .	should we do this?
Every morning	before filling the cups, they should be emptied, cleaned in hot water and dried.
Every evening	take out food waste and leftover greens. Remove the soiled parts of the sand with a spoon. Clean dirty perches with sandpaper. Replace bedding when necessary.
During the molt, several times a week	remove loose feathers from the cage.
At least twice a week	clean cage, perches, and toys. Replace all bedding.
Weekly	clean the bird tree and cage bottom. Remove droppings and other dirt.
Monthly or when necessary	replace branches from cage and bird tree with fresh ones. Add new sand for the bird tree.

The Right Care

Personal hygiene takes up a major part of the bird's time, because only a bird with perfect plumage is fast and agile enough to outfly enemies (see page 48), but budgies *create* some dirt so hygiene is very important. The cage, the bird tree, and all accessories have to be kept clean (washing, vacuuming) to keep the birds healthy (see page 55).

Important: Don't use detergents or cleansers for cleaning the cage or anything the bird comes in contact with, as the chemicals in them are toxic to the birds. Clean water about 130°F (55°C) is quite adequate and presents no danger.

This budgie is enjoying the luxury of a bath in a flowerpot coaster.

Cleaning the Cage

The cage, bird tree, and all other objects the bird uses or touches have to be kept meticulously clean if your pet is to remain free of pests and parasites and other harmful influences (see page 58). At least once a week the cage, and its bottom pan, which holds the sand tray, should be washed with hot water. You may let a tame bird free in the room (see page 25) or place it in another cage until you have finished. Remember the following:

1. At least twice a week all dirty perches, cups, and toys should be scrubbed with a small metal brush, rinsed with hot water, and dried thoroughly.

2. Use hot water for cleaning. Cleaners and chemical rinses are harmful and possibly even fatal for birds.

3. Wash out and dry the bottom of the cage weekly.

4. Wash and brush the bars of the cage weekly.

5. Discard leftover birdseed at least once a week.

6. Replace chewed branches when necessary (see page 18). Don't forget to wash and dry the fresh replacements.

7. Clean gravel on the bottom of the cage is not only hygienic, but is also important for the health of the bird. It will pick up a little gravel every day to aid digestion. Special bird gravel and oyster shell mixes also supply calcium and other minerals.

When a Bird Escapes

Six out of ten pet parakeets escape at some point. That is a disheartening statistic if you keep in mind that in certain climates in the country, the birds have no chance of survival. To make things worse, budgies are unable to make use of landmarks to help them orient themselves, as it is an ability they have no need

Checklist
A Clean Cage

1 Are food and drinking cups clean and dry?

2 Are rotting fruits and greens immediately removed?

3 Are the bottom of the cage and the perches free of droppings?

4 Is fresh drinking water available? Replace dirty water immediately, and dry the area around the cup regularly to prevent mold, which is harmful to the birds.

5 Are gravel, sand, bedding, and bird tree dry and clean?

6 Are all toys, ropes (see page 53) and dishes dry and clean?

7 Are all branches still fresh? Replace chewed ones immediately.

A good relationship will prolong the lives of both birds.

for in their original nomadic life in Australia. For this reason, a lost budgie never finds its way back home and will die unless it happens to be found and taken in by someone. Therefore, the first and foremost rule for any budgie owner is to keep doors and windows closed at all times. A budgie can escape even from a closed cage by squeezing through the crack of the drawer opening if the sand tray is left out for a moment, or it may learn to open the cage door with its strong beak. Curtains in front of an open window offer no protection against escape either because the bird may climb up on them, wend its way snakelike through the narrow space between two curtain rings, and take off. That is why at least one window in the bird

room should have a strong metal screen with spaces between the wires no larger than ³/₈ by ³/₈ inch (1 × 1 cm). The screen should be mounted on a wooden frame that fits tightly into the window opening so that you won't have to worry about airing the room and you can let the bird live in it without constant supervision.

What can we do if the bird escapes? If the bird is still in the neighborhood, place a cage (or its cage) in your yard, with another budgie in it. The bird calls will lure the escapee back to its cage. A tame budgie will quickly jump on your hand. If your bird is not trained, place the cage close to an open window, with its partner inside.

If you cannot find your bird, place an ad in your local paper, and ask friends and neighbors for assistance.

Stages of Life of a Budgie

Dogs, cats, and budgerigars all can enjoy a long life—15 to 20 years. For dogs or cats, their first two years are years of fun and play, clearly their youth. Budgies, however, at that age are already full grown; their youth last two to three months!

During their youth, budgerigars like to play at all hours of the day. They are very inquisitive and playful, hang upside down on their perches, and run in little circles. This is the time that they will look for company and attention—ideal time for training and taming (see page 22).

Full-grown budgies are about three months old. If they have a partner, they will start raising a family.

Senior citizens are birds that don't breed anymore and are near the end of their lives. They are not as active as when they were raising a family. Be good to them; their care remains the same as when they were young.

VACATION TIME

If you would like to go away on vacation you have to make plans not just for yourself but also for your bird.

Vacations abroad are out of the question for budgies because entry regulations applying to members of the parrot family are so stringent.

A trip by car is possible, but if the budgie goes along, you have to make sure there are no drafts in the car during hot summer weather. If you stay in a hotel or motel, the bird has to stay inside its cage to prevent its escape.

Staying at home is the best alternative for the bird.

Ask a friend or relative to look after the bird and talk and play with it twice a day.

Give written instructions and leave a phone number where your caretaker can reach you.

Sometimes pet stores or veterinary offices board birds for a small fee.

Wherever you leave your bird, always have enough of its familiar food available.

UNDERSTANDING BUDGERIGARS

It is a joy to study and observe budgerigars. They are not only inventive in their behavior but also adorable parents as they take care of their young.

Observing Birds

When you have domestic birds, you will notice that the male will declare his love, although at the start he is rather cautious around the hen. Gradually he moves next to her and eagerly taps his beak against hers. She in turn hacks at him less and less frequently to keep him at a distance. Budgies mate for life, but it is not always love at first sight. If you see two birds touch beaks and preen each other, sooner or later, you will see them get ready to mate.

Mating Dance

The posture of a budgie hen ready to mate is almost coquettish. A hen that is interested in a male will approach him in a slightly bent-over posture and let him feed her. In his growing sexual excitement the male tries to step on the female's tail; she responds by whirling around instantly and protesting vociferously. The male now tries to impress his mate. He pulls on the

bell in the cage with all his might, making it swing madly around his head, circles around the room in rapid flight, approaches the hen again to give her a gentle nudge with his beak, then runs up and down in front of her excitedly, nodding and bowing continually. He keeps talking the entire time and makes the feathers on his throat and forehead stand on end. His eyes take on their typical courtship look with the pupils contracting into tiny dots. The female doesn't seem to be overly impressed by all this attention.

Breeding Season

At some point the hen will indicate her readiness to mate in a charming gesture: She raises her tail straight up and throws her head back, then she remains motionless in this graceful pose.

The male, in apparent confusion, alternates between putting one foot on her back and touching beaks with her until he has gathered the courage to mount her. Holding onto the neck feathers of the female, he holds one or both wings around her and presses his cloaca against hers so that his semen can get to her oviduct.

A budgie pair don't mind if you watch their courtship.

Nest Box

To help your birds get into a reproductive mood, place a nest box in the cage or in the bird tree. You can buy commercial nest boxes measuring 10 inches × 6 inches × 6 inches (25 cm × 15 cm × 15 cm). In the wall of the longer side there is an entrance hole with a perch below it. Inside the box there is a block with a hollow in it. The top of the box flips open for easy checking of the nest and the nestlings. At first, the birds respond to the nest with irritation and avoid it, but the female eventually approaches it hesitantly and peeks through the entrance hole. Soon she gets brave enough to slip in for a moment, then she starts working inside the box, chipping at the hollow in the block to make it deeper. She stays inside the box a bit longer every day, letting the male feed her but normally refusing to let him in. If a male budgie persists and penetrates the box anyway, this is a phenomenon due to domestication; in the wild, the female would never permit this.

The female deposits the first egg about eight days after the mating. Before laying the first egg, young females sometimes make themselves sleek and slender and spread their wings, trembling. The droppings at this time get runnier and are passed in greater amounts. The cere above the bill becomes lighter in color and smoother than before. If the first egg drops to the floor because the nest box wasn't ready, the female has a hard time maintaining her balance on the perch. Shaking, she fans out the feathers on her wings, which are raised high, and bites into the empty air. After a few minutes, she recovers. If there is no nest box, no further attention is paid to the egg, or it may be destroyed. If the hen has deposited her first egg inside the nest box, however, she rarely emerges from the box because she begins to sit on the egg right away. She keeps on laying an egg every other day until there is a clutch of three to five, rarely more. The baby birds will later hatch in the same order and at the same intervals as the eggs were laid. The eggs of a budgie weigh 2 grams, exactly the same as a newly hatched chick.

A Chick Hatches

The process of hatching takes about 20 minutes. Some chicks are apparently unable to turn in the egg and therefore peck only a small hole in the shell. These chicks are not strong enough to break open the shell and would perish if the mother didn't come to their aid by breaking off more of the shell until the chick can finally emerge. The mother bird now leaves the nest box only three or four times a day to defecate. She is fed exclusively by the male and sticks her head out of the entrance hole only to get food. Even though the male stays close by, keeping guard and reassuring his mate with songs and short calls, the female checks out the situation with quick glances at the slightest unusual sound.

During the first few days, the chicks lie on their backs while being fed.

During copulation, the male wraps one wing around the hen.

About 24 hours before hatching, the chick starts making chirping and cracking sounds, a signal for the mother to check the eggs more frequently. She gets up and feels the surface of the eggs with her tongue, looking for the first holes in the shell. The chick pecks against the shell with its egg tooth; then it turns a fraction of an inch and pecks again, creating a small crack in the thin shell. After a lot of painstaking hard work—pecking, turning, craning the neck—half the shell flips open like the hinged lid of a box. With further stretching, now of the wings and legs, the hatchling finally emerges completely. Keep the following in mind:

✔ During the breeding season, the hen wants to hear her mate near the nest box, but commotion, noise, and other disturbing activities in the room can bother her enough to make her stop laying or brooding, especially during the first few days.

✔ Once the hen has settled down on the eggs, she is less easily upset, and you can occasionally lift the cover and peek into the nest box without a problem.

✔ Remove infertile eggs after approximately ten days of incubation (hold the egg up to a light; infertile eggs appear light and translucent) but only when there are more than four he clutch. Too great a change might irritate the hen and cause her to cease brooding. For healthy development of the embryos, a steady temperature of about 72°F (22°C), fresh air, and a humidity level of 60 percent are important. To achieve the right humidity, you can set up a humidifier, or you can simply place a large bowl of water, covered by a wire screen, in the room.

The Development of Budgie Chicks

At first, budgie chicks are totally naked, blind, and so weak that they cannot even raise their heads, and crane them toward the mother to beg for food. They are entirely dependent on the mother bird for survival but they develop very quickly once they have hatched. Young budgies are ready to fly at four weeks, and two months later they are already capable of reproducing. They grow rapidly and reach the adult weight of about 30 grams on the sixteenth or seventeenth day. In the following days they gain a little more but lose this extra weight again by the time they leave the nest box. The eyes open on the sixth or seventh day. On the seventh day the primary feathers begin to appear, and on the ninth day, the

tail feathers. The down covering is complete after ten to eleven days. By the time the birds are four to five weeks old—the time when they are ready to leave the nest box—the large wing feathers have grown to three-quarters of their full length and the tail feathers two-thirds. The young are already good fliers. In another seven to ten days the flight feathers are as long as they are going to be.

As the nestlings prepare to leave the nest box, they'll keep a lookout at the entrance hole and often flutter about in the box to exercise their flight muscles. As you watch them crowd to the entrance and get ready to fly, give them every opportunity to try out their wings. If the nest box is in the cage, keep the cage door open. The young birds' first attempts at flight are more fluttering than flying. Landing is difficult for them, so they'll need your help. A few lengths of rope stretched across the room and some branches stuck into pots of soil around the area will provide handy landing places for the birds as they venture farther from the nest.

Feeding Chicks

Nestlings do not need any special feed if the diet they usually get contains all the necessary nutrients (see page 30). As the chicks get older, the feeding pattern changes. From about the eighth day, the nestlings are hardly fed at all at night, even if they beg for food. From the age of about ten to twelve days the chicks start sitting up for the entire

The first feathers are visible but sitting up straight still takes some doing.

feeding and no longer lie flat on their backs while being fed (see photo, page 40). After three weeks, the nestlings start wandering about in the nest box and follow the mother, begging for food. They are able to aim their beaks at the mother, and their begging now takes the form of jerking jabs at the food. The mother feeds her three-week-old offspring not only when they beg, but when she is ready, for instance, when she returns to the nest box.

Sometimes the parents won't feed their chicks enough, or will neglect them altogether. To make sure your chicks are getting enough to eat, carefully feel their crops, the throat area beneath the bill, with your thumb and forefinger. If the crops feel empty and you can see that the chicks are not developing normally, you'll have to play the role of parent and feed them yourself.

At your pet supply store, purchase a feeding syringe and food specially formulated for nestlings. Until the fourteenth day of life, feed the baby birds with the syringe. Place a chick on a piece of soft paper towel and with the syringe drip the nestling food onto its tongue until the crop is full, but not stuffed. Gently clean the chick with a damp paper towel and place it back in the nest box. Repeat the feeding several times a day. After the chicks are fourteen days old, feem them with a baby spoon or demitasse spoon.

Breeders should be satisfied with two clutches a year. Start breeding in March or (when you have garden aviaries) the end of April. It is risky to start early in areas in which it is bitter cold in the spring. The last of the chicks have to be ready to leave the nest at the end of August or early September. The molting season starts then for the parents, and they should not have to worry about tending to young ones at that time.

TIP

Observing Chicks

If you like to watch the entire process of a budgie chick's growing up, use a nest box with a glass back and install a video camera in such a way that it does not disturb the birds. When not observing, cover the back with a black cloth. Before you begin observing the birds, be sure that the lights are correctly adjusted. If you don't use a video camera, the room has to be dim. Don't observe for more than ten minutes at a time.

BEHAVIOR
EXPLAINED

Budgies express many feelings to humans and other birds, with their pronounced body language.

☞ *The budgie's behavior.*

❓ *What does the budgie want to tell me?*

❗ *The correct response to the budgie's behavior.*

☞ A hen puts her head under her partner's beak.

❓ She loves to be groomed on the head. The chatting strengthens their relationship.

❗ You have to scratch a singleton carefully with your finger.

☞ Budgies climb through the branches on their bellies.

❓ They love to play.

❗ Offer them lots of playing room.

☞ The bird raises its wings.

❓ It is getting a little overheated and now gives off some body heat.

❗ Let the budgie sit in the shade.

☞ The male feeds the female.

❓ She feeds and raises the chicks.

❗ Offer the proper food.

☞ The budgie rubs its beak and head against its perch.

❓ It wants to clean its beak and keep it in proper shape.

❗ Clean perches regularly.

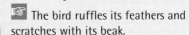

☞ The bird ruffles its feathers and scratches with its beak.

❓ Budgies spend several hours a day preening their plumage.

❗ If they are scratching noticeably more, they might be infested with parasites.

he hen moves her ☞ head backwards while beak-tapping.

s is a sure sign for ❓ the male to copulate with her.

f you want young, ❗ supply a nest box.

☞ The newcomer is greeted with open beak.

❓ There is jealousy at the dish of greens.

❗ Offer various feeding places if you have more than one bird.

☞ The budgie pecks with its beak under its raised wing.

❓ It is caring for its flight feathers.

❗ Offer the bird enough room to fly free.

Social Behavior

Among budgerigars, everything from courtship and mating to the selection of nesting sites, raising young, and introducing juvenile birds into the flock—as well as all interactions within the flock, including even aggression—is regulated by universally understood patterns of behavior that are typical of the species.

Head Scratching

One of the birds sits erect and gently works over the head and neck region of the partner that deliberately turns and offers areas of slightly ruffled plumage for scratching. Sometimes the bird that is having its head scratched jerks back suddenly with a short cry, although clearly having a good time.

✔ Head scratching releases stress and strengthens the immune system; the birds,

The best opportunity to study budgies' behavior is when they are kept in small flocks.

therefore, become less susceptible to diseases (see page 55).
✔ It calms the birds.
✔ It strengthen the bonds between partners.
✔ It has a useful hygienic function (cleaning of feathers).

Vocal Utterances

Contact call: This call helps the birds stay in touch with each other. Birds also recognize each other individually by their calls.
Alarm call: Parakeets warn the flock with a short, shrill call when they spot a bird of prey or some other danger. Cage birds can also produce this call.

Murmur: At dusk and after the flock has gathered in the treetops, a murmur call (*"eeaye"*) can be heard, followed by a soft chirping.

Aggressive Behavior

There is no evidence so far that budgies have an aggression-inhibiting mechanism such as the one we see in dogs. Tense body posture and threatening vocal utterances are used by parakeets to express displeasure. The bird that evoked the aggressive response usually flies away.

Threatening gesture: This is often seen when two birds are an equal match. The threatening bird:

✔ approaches the other bird with open beak,
✔ plants its foot on its opponent's chest,
✔ flattens its feathers.

Fights: There is little cause for concern where a pair have adjusted to each other because males hardly ever attack females. Fights can arise, however, if we inadvertently or thoughtlessly add a second hen to an established pair.

Checklist
Observations

1 When a budgie turns its head backwards and tucks it into the back feathers, it is in a sleeping posture.

2 A budgie that shows its neck to its partner likes to be preened.

3 When two birds feed each other, there is a deep affection between them.

4 If two birds are an equal match and stand tall, with flattened feathers, they are making a threatening gesture.

5 Birds try to impress each other with raised wings. To reduce heat loss, they huddle close together with puffed feathers (insulating barrier).

6 If a budgie is squatting apathetically on its perch with half-shut eyes, ruffled feathers, a drooping tail, and in an almost horizontal position, it is sick and must be seen by an avian veterinarian.

Typical Daily Behavior

In the wild, a budgie spends several hours a day preening its plumage. Obviously, it is not constantly grooming itself, but almost any activity—feeding, sleeping, or doing something with a partner—ends up with a few minutes of preening. Only a bird whose plumage is smooth, clean, and lightly oiled is totally in command of its full flying powers.

Commotion

In their natural environment, huge flocks of several thousand birds descend onto the open grassland in the early morning and late after-noon to feed. Budgies hardly ever do anything individually; they do almost everything in the company of others. Therefore, budgies should be kept in pairs or in small flocks. A common commotion with young birds is the vigorous flapping of their wings while holding on tight to the perch they are sitting on. This is a way of exercising the wing muscles. Adult budgies also flap their wings if they haven't had a chance to fly around.

Grooming

When preening itself, a bird runs its feathers through its beak one at a time, smoothing each one and ridding each one of even the smallest dirt particles and tiny flakes that are left from the sheaths of new feathers. With acrobatic skill, budgies twist and turn to run even the long tail and flight feathers through the beak. The smallest contour feathers are groomed in what often looks like frantic activity—breast, belly, legs, underside wings, and back all get their turn. Even the naked

Lift up my foot, push off, and climb up to the other hand . . .

feet and toes are attended to with the beak, and all dirt and skin particles removed. Budgies have an oil gland (uropygial gland) containing a fatty substance that is located on the lower back. The bird frequently rubs its head over this gland, oiling the head feathers and beak. It then distributes this fat evenly over individual feathers, feet, and toes. The oil protects the feathers from drying out in heat and wind and also protects them against rain.

Sleeping and Resting

In their homeland, parakeets gather in trees to sleep. Caged budgies, also, retreat at dusk to specific sleeping places in the cage or aviary. In contrast to wild birds, which sleep in different places every night, most pet birds keep the same sleeping place for years.

The rhythm of sleep and waking hours is related to the position of the sun in the sky. Our caged birds follow a certain daily rhythm, whether dictated by the

sun, changes of temperature, or external care-taking routines. A dozing budgie sits quietly with closed eyes, slightly puffed feathers, and one leg drawn up into the plumage on the abdomen. The bird assumes the same posture in deep sleep but also turns its head back and tucks its bill into the back feathers.

The Senses

Sight: Budgies, like all birds, have a much larger field of vision than humans; they also see the world in colors. Since their eyes are on the sides of the head and register images independently of each other, birds see not only what is going on in front and on the sides, but to a considerable extent also what is approaching from behind. This offers the birds a constant panoramic view of their surroundings without having to turn their heads, and it helps them spot a potential enemy and escape. Because its eyes are placed on the sides of the head, however, a parakeet has a considerably smaller range of spatial vision (the

area that both eyes take in at once) than humans do. On the other hand, a bird's eye can register up to 150 images per second compared to the human eye's limit of about 16.

Hearing: Most birds have a very acute sense of hearing because calls and songs are a major form of avian communication. Budgies have a better memory for specific frequencies (such as shrill alarm cries) and are also better than we are at analyzing acoustic signals. What sounds to us like amorphous shrieking is a clearly recognizable sequence of sound that a bird can reproduce exactly.

Smell and taste: So far there have been no conclusive studies about the budgie's ability to smell. According to many fanciers, their pets' special preferences would indicate that budgies do respond to taste, but other studies in this respect are conclusive.

Touch: By means of specialized cells in the legs—the so-called Herbst corpuscles or touch receptors—birds are able to receive even the most minute vibrations of their perches. This is very important to survival because the ability to sense vibrations warns the birds of impending natural events or of an enemy's approach, and also serves as a cue for flight. Make sure, therefore, that the permanent location of the cage is absolutely free of vibration. Never put the cage down on a refrigerator, for instance, even for a few minutes; in its flight reaction, the bird might seriously hurt itself.

. . . can we play climbing-the-stairs again?

The 10 Most Popular Games
for Budgerigars

1 Attach some wooden clothespins to the cage. The birds like to pull at them, sit on them, and nibble at them.

2 Fill a plastic dish with 1 inch (3 cm) of water. Put some floating fruit (grapes, for example) into the dish and put the bird on the rim of the dish. He will push the fruits back and forth, trying to grip them.

3 Put your bird on your shoulder and whistle a tune that it will be able to imitate.

4 Fasten a string to the middle of a branch and attach the branch to the bird's cage or bird tree so that it can move back and forth. Soon two birds will land on it and start swinging.

5 Put similar pieces of cardboard on top of various dishes of different sizes. Put water in one, millet spray in an other, and so on. The bird will soon know where to look for "the good stuff."

6 Attach a bell on the bird tree. Tie a string to the clapper. The bird will eventually take the string and ring the bell.

7 Place some marbles on the table. The bird will push them against one another and enjoy the noise and movement.

8 Wrap a small piece of millet spray in paper and make a ball. Birds love to play with this! After a while, the wrapping will come loose, and the bird will find its reward.

9 If your budgie is extremely tame, put it on your hand and carefully bring him to a slowly running faucet (cold water, of course). It will go into the water, and enjoy a shower.

10 Fasten various colorful wooden beads on a round perch or wire. Place this "calculator" in the bird's cage. It doesn't know how to count, but it certainly knows how to play.

Games and Activities

Budgies are one of the most intelligent birds we know. They need no special encouragement to start whistling, imitating sounds, or saying words they hear a lot, but interest, intelligence, and talent for mimicry vary from budgie to budgie.

Do Budgies Talk?

If a budgie shows talent and an interest in talking, it is because it wants to "have its say" in the company of humans (its new flock) and because it wants to belong. A parakeet that is interested in talking will sit in the hand of its human friend, edging as close as possible to the person's mouth and listening, entranced, to the words spoken. If the person is a patient teacher, the budgie keeps learning new words and combinations. The bird likes to hear repeatedly the expressions it already knows, and as new words are introduced to the vocabulary the bird has already mastered, they are eagerly tried out and repeated. If this special intimacy between bird and human remains undisturbed, the budgie is likely to learn the new words without becoming distracted.

Toys and Other Fun Objects

For a singleton budgie, toys often serve less as toys than as a surrogate partner. What your budgie needs for play more than anything else is your company as well as a partner. Budgies spend a surprising amount of time picking away at fresh branches (such as willow) and playing with objects (see pages 50 and 52). These objects don't always have to be toys; anything that makes the birds move around and occupies them in different ways is fine.

*I love to fling my ball
into her hand!*

Intelligence Test

Budgies can count to three—at least. Construct a cardboard box (see box at right) and, instead of coloring each side with a different color, paint one, two, or three dots on the panels. Hide some food behind the panel that has three dots on it. The birds will be very excited while playing this; it is hard to see what is more important to them, the food or the action.

The trick is to find the card with the three dots.

After the search comes the reward. That tastes good!

Hide and Seek

Budgies are able to see colors.

1. Put millet spray in one of two similar dishes.

2. Place a green piece of construction paper over the first dish; over the second one, which is empty, place a red paper.

3. Show the bird an extra green piece of paper.

4. The bird will understand and walk over to the dish with the green board.

5. It then will move the board aside and will find the food dish.

Stimulating Play

Wild budgies are equipped with intelligence, physical agility, and excellent flying skills, but all this potential lies idle in a pet budgie. A healthy budgie shows an interest in vocal mimicry and inventive play, and has great curiosity.

Ropes with Treats

It doesn't take much to make a budgie happy. Interaction will strengthen its health and curiosity.

✔ Place various ropes in the bird room (horizontally, perpendicularly, and so on). All birds, especially youngsters, love to swing on them.

✔ Don't forget to change the rope arrangement often.

✔ Occasionally, attach bells, rings, millet spray, and swings to these ropes.

Bathing

Budgies love to take baths (see page 18). If the bird doesn't approach the bathhouse, place some properly rinsed and still moist parsley,

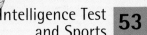

It's really fun to play among these ropes.

young dandelion greens, or spinach in it. Many budgies prefer this kind of "dew bath."

Think Ahead

No two budgies are the same. The following intelligence test will prove this:

The budgie is dunking its belly and wings in water.

1. Place a cage that is not familiar to the birds in the middle of the bird room and put millet spray on top of the cage. During this test, all the food from the birds' own cage should be removed.

2. The birds will land on the roof of the cage and begin to munch on the millet spray. As soon as the birds are used to finding their treat on top of the cage, the real test begins.

3. Put the millet spray inside the cage, leaving one side door open. Out of habit, the birds will land on the roof but will not find any food. The "I-don't-care" birds will nibble somewhat at the mesh but will soon leave the area. The bright ones, however, will look for an opening to get to the food. They will soon discover the open door and then the food.

4. In order to be sure that this is not pure luck, open the second cage door. The same birds that found the food the first time will also find it this time.

IF YOUR BIRD GETS SICK

Proper cage care and everyday management will prevent the bird from getting sick, but it is important to know what a healthy budgie looks like. Don't hesitate to take the bird to the veterinarian if it shows any sign of illness.

Prevention Is Better than Cure

A bird in top physical condition is more likely to survive if an illness does strike, therefore, be sure to commit to memory the following list of what is good for the birds and what is bad for them.

A parakeet needs: Fresh and not chemically treated fruit and vegetables, a varied diet, fresh drinking water, natural, unsprayed branches, regular playtime, free flight in a well-aired room, physical closeness with the owner, and strict cleanliness.

Harmful are: Sudden temperature fluctuations, drafts, rotting food or food treated with chemicals, food intended for humans, poisonous plants, exposure to direct sunlight, rooms with impure air (containing tobacco smoke or toxic or caustic fumes), loneliness.

A Sick Budgie

A sick bird usually sits on its favorite perch apathetically, its plumage puffed up, and its tail

These budgies are active and healthy due to proper care and lots of love.

drooping slightly. It avoids all contact. Often, the beak is tucked into the back feathers, the eyes are half shut, and the bird rests on both legs, not on one as a healthy bird sleeps. It stares into space with dull eyes; it hardly eats anything, but drinks a great deal. If such a sick bird is not treated promptly, it soon loses so much strength that it can barely balance on the perch and rests almost directly on its abdomen or lies flat on the cage floor. Don't hesitate too long to take the bird to the veterinarian, for such a small creature needs help quickly.

How to Help a Sick Bird

Make sure the bird's room is very quiet, and provide warmth. A sick bird needs a cage of its own and should be given lukewarm chamomile tea to drink. Sometimes the use of an infrared lamp also helps. When using such a lamp, cover half the cage with a cloth, so that the bird can get away from the lamp's rays if it gets too hot.

A sick bird will stir around in the food dish with its beak but will hardly eat any seeds or pellets. Often, the bird will seem to be exceptionally thirsty.

The Visit to the Veterinarian

If your bird's condition does not improve within a few hours, you should take it to an avian veterinarian on the same day or, at the very latest, the next day. If you notice any sign of alarm (see page 59), you must consult a veterinarian immediately. In many cities, veterinarians can be reached even at night and on holidays in an emergency, but veterinarians rarely make house calls; usually, you have to take your bird to them. Replace the sand in the bottom of the cage with clean paper so that the veterinarian can immediately tell the consistency of the droppings. Protect the bird against cold, dampness, and high temperatures on the way to the office. It *is* best to put a cover on the cage or

If your budgie sits on its perch with half-closed eyes and drooping tail, like the bird on the left, take it to the veterinarian.

carry it in a big box, but make sure that there is sufficient air circulation.

Molt

The molt is not a disease, but for somewhat older budgies it is a period of increased physical strain, during which the birds should get especially nutritious food and be kept warm in a quiet environment. The molt is a natural process, during which all birds replace their feathers. Before the molt and during this process, the bird needs constant warmth, proper air, humidity, quiet, and a diet that is rich in vitamins and minerals (sprouted kernels, fresh greens, fruit, cuttlebone, and so on).

Overgrown Claws

In older and frail birds, the toenails sometimes grow excessively long, in extreme cases even curling like a corkscrew. The usual explanation is that the claws do not get enough wear on artificial perches that are smooth and too thin and do not allow for enough exercise. Since claws that are too long hamper and endanger a bird (catching in fabrics or in a chain, getting stuck in cracks, impeding grooming), the toenails have to be cut. Hold the nail against the light so that you can clearly see the dark blood vessels. Don't cut into the quick and try not to have the claw splinter. Some pet stores offer free claw and bill trimming to their customers.

Excessive Beak Growth

The beak sometimes grows too fast, especially in older budgies (for reasons not yet known), in spite of frequent whetting. Usually only the upper mandible is affected, but more rarely the upper and lower mandibles cross each other because they both grow too long simultaneously. In either case, the bird's intake of food is hampered. So don't let things get that far. It is recommended that you take the bird to an avian veterinarian, breeder, or pet dealer to have the beak trimmed with proper (nail) clippers. If the bird has a predisposition for excessive beak growth, regular trimming may be necessary, sometimes as often as every four weeks.

Egg Binding

Egg binding is the term given to the difficulty in laying eggs and especially to the inability of a bird to press the egg out of the oviduct and vent.

Checklist
Preventing Illnesses

1 A budgie that is kept singly is not a complete budgie and is very susceptible to diseases.

2 A budgie should have the opportunity to fly for at least an hour two or three times a day.

3 Vitamins and variety in food will help to prevent illness.

4 Keep the cage and bird tree as clean as possible.

5 Avoid drafts and dampness at all cost, as well as sudden temperature fluctuations.

6 Give your bird a sunbath once in a while (for vitamin D). Avoid exposure to direct sunshine if there is no shady retreat. Stay with the bird and watch out for cats and other predators. Keep your bird caged at all times, because budgies love to take flight and don't know how to find their way back home.

Measures to take: Try to provide relief with damp heat, or drip some warm castor oil or salad oil on the vent with an eyedropper every ten minutes. If the egg is not produced within two hours, take the bird to the veterinarian.

Parasites

Ectoparasites such as red mites, feather mites, and lice are often the reason for prolonged loss of feathers, bald spots, and rough-looking plumage. Mites attack birds of all ages. Notorious is the red mite that lives on blood that it sucks from the birds. This mite is active at night and can cause your birds great discomfort. Many commercial insecticides are effective against red mites and other parasites. Most of them contain pyrethrin, which is harmless to birds. Follow the instructions and clean all cages, perches, and nest boxes, as well as your birds (housed temporarily in clean cages). Treat the birds with pyrethrin (or carbaryl), with special attention to the neck, the area around the cloaca, and under the wings.

Contagious Diseases

Psittacosis: This disease is difficult to diagnose. Most affected birds are apathetic, pass droppings that are too soft and often contain traces of blood, have the sniffles, and are short of breath, or the disease may manifest itself in conjunctivitis and slimy secretions at the lower eyelids. All these symptoms can occur singly or in combination; it is therefore important to watch the bird carefully. Take the bird to the veterinarian immediately, as humans can be infected. Drugs have been developed that effectively cure the disease in birds as well as in humans if it is treated in good time.

French molt, also known as *budgerigar fledgling disease,* is seen in young birds, four to six weeks old. They are often called runners or creepers because they have retarded growth and poor feathering so that they cannot fly. A polyomavirus is suspected but not definitely confirmed. At this time, no good remedy has been found. It goes without saying that creepers should never be used for breeding.

Walking up and down a perch helps keep your budgie's nails short.

When to Consult an Avian Veterinarian

What Is Different?	Symptoms
Activity	• The bird is sleepy, inactive, or apathetic. • It has a staring expression. • It leaves the others, often hiding in a corner.
Appetite	• The bird eats more or less than usual. • It drinks more water than usual. • It tries to get rid of mucus.
Digestion	• The bird defecates less than usual (count the droppings). • Droppings are watery, sometimes with blood or other coloring.
Plumage	• Plumage is ruffled and dull. • The tail is drooping. • Bare spots appear in the sparse plumage, particularly on the head and the undersides of the wings.
Wing	• The bird stretches its wing.
Breathing	• The bird has difficulty breathing. • Squeaking or rattling noises are sometimes produced. • The bird coughs up food.
Eyes	• The eyes are inflamed or swollen.
Nose	• The bird has a runny nose. • Discoloration of the cere (from blue to brown) can be seen.
Abdomen	• The abdomen is swollen.

Fractures

A bird may break a leg by getting its toes entangled, crashing to the ground during free flight, or enduring some other misfortune. The injured leg hangs down uselessly. A broken wing also hangs uselessly, and grounds the bird. Put the patient in a cage without perches and consult an avian veterinarian immediately. Cuts and similar injuries require no medical treatment. Simply dab lukewarm chamomile tea on the injured area and press coagulant cotton against it until the bleeding stops. If there is considerable loss of blood (a damaged blood vessel, for example) consult a veterinarian as soon as possible.

60 I N D E X

The salad is not just for snacking. It also provides a moist bath.

Useful Addresses

American Budgerigar Society
141 Hill Street Extension
Naugatuck, CT 06770

American Federation of
Aviculture
P.O. Box 56218
Phoenix, AZ 85079

Aviculture Society of America
P.O. Box 5516
Riverside, CA 92517

The Avicultural Society of
Queensland
c/o Mr. Ray Garwood
19 Fahey's Road
Albany Creek, 4035, Queensland
Australia

Bird Clubs of America
P.O. Box 2005
Yorktown, VA 23692

The Budgerigar Society
(England)
57, Stephyn's Chambers
Bank Cour
Marlowes, Hemel Hempstead,
Herts
England

The Golden Triangle Parrot
Club
P.O. Box 1574, Station C
Kitchener, Ontario
Canada, N2G 4P2

Great Western Budgie Society
9428 Blackley Street
Temple City, CA 91780

International Aviculturists
Society
P.O. Box 280383
Memphis, TN 38168

National Cage Bird Show Club
4910 Antony Lane
Pasadena, TX 77504

Books

Birmelin, Immanuel, and
Annette Wolter. *The New
Parakeet Handbook,*
Hauppauge, New York:
Barron's Educational Series,
Inc., 1986.
Piers, Helen. *How to Take Care
of Your Parakeet.* Hauppauge,
New York: Barron's
Educational Series, Inc., 1993.
Vriends, Dr. Matthew M. *The
Complete Budgerigar.* New
York, New York: Howell Book
House, 1985.
——. *The New Bird Handbook.*
Hauppauge, New York:
Barron's Educational Series,
Inc., 1989.
——. *Hand-Feeding and Raising
Baby Birds.* Hauppauge, New
York: Barron's Educational
Series, Inc., 1996.

Wolter, Annette and Monika
Wegler. *The Complete Book
of Parakeet Care.*
Hauppauge, New York:
Barron's Educational Series,
Inc., 1994.

Magazines

The AFA Watchbird
American Federation of
Aviculture
3118 West Thomas Road
Suite 713
Phoenix, AZ 85017

Bird Talk
P.O. Box 57437
Boulder, CO 80323

Birds USA
P.O. Box 55811
Boulder, CO 80322

Budgerigar World (England)
County Press Buildings
Bala, North Wales, LL23 7PG
England

*Cage and Aviary Birds
(England)*
Prospect House
9-15 Ewell Road
Cheam, Sutton, Surrey SM3 8B2
England

About the Author

Dr. Immanuel Birmelin is a biologist and ornithologist at the University of Bern, Switzerland. For his doctoral thesis he studied budgerigars intensively and wrote about the hatching of parakeet chicks and the behavior of the mother birds. Dr. Birmelin has been raising budgies successfully for many years and still devotes a major portion of his scientific studies to these popular small parrots.

About the Photographers

Most pictures were taken by Uwe Anders. He is a biology teacher and author, but he is famous for his beautiful nature pictures which are published in various books and magazines. He has illustrated many *Complete Pet Owner's Manuals* for Barron's Educational Series, Inc.

Other photographers who have pictures in this book are: Arendt and Schweiger: pages 10, 11; Juniors/Aschermann: small picture cover 1; Neukamp: page 37; Wegler: cover 2/1, 2/3, 4/5, 6/7, 16, 17, 18, 21, 24, 29, 31, 32, 48, 49, 50 (large picture).

About the Illustrator

György Jankovics studied graphic art at the Academy of Arts in Budapest and Hamburg. He is the illustrator of many of Barron's pet books.

Important Note

This book deals with the care and maintenance of budgerigars. People who are allergic to feathers or feather dust should not keep birds. If you are not sure whether you might have such an allergy, consult a doctor before buying birds.

When birds are handled, they sometimes bite and scratch. Have such wounds immediately treated by a physician.

At this time, psittacosis is very rare in parakeets, but if it occurs it is extremely dangerous both in birds and humans. If you have any reason to suspect psittacosis, take your bird to the veterinarian for examination, and if you have flu or cold symptoms, consult your doctor and mention that you keep birds.

Original title of the book in German is *Wellensittiche*.

Copyright © 1997 by Gräfe und Unzer Verlag GmbH, Munich.

All inquiries should be addressed to:
Barron's Educational Series, Inc.
250 Wireless Boulevard
Hauppauge, New York 11788

http://www.barronseduc.com

Library of Congress Catalog Card No. 98-20371

International Standard Book Number 0-7641-0662-7

Library of Congress Cataloging-in-Publication Data
Birmelin, I. (Immanuel)
[Wellensittiche. English]
Budgerigars / with color photographs by Uwe Anders and other animal photographers ; illustrations by György Jankovics ; translated and adapted by Matthew M. Vriends.
p. cm. — (A complete pet owner's manual)
Includes bibliographical references and index.
ISBN 0-7641-0662-7
1. Budgerigars. I. Title. II. Series.
SF473.B8B57413 1998
636.6′864—dc21 98-20371
CIP

Printed in Hong Kong

987654

most common
ns about budgerigars.

1 Should I purchase one or two budgies?

2 How often should I offer my budgie free flight in the bird room?

3 It is possible to teach budgies to talk?

4 How did they get the name "budgerigar"?

5 How does the budgie get its various colors?

6 What is the best way to keep my budgie's nails short?

7 What does it mean when budgies flap their wings?

8 How much should my budgie eat?

9 Which of the budgie's organs is the most active?

10 What is the most frequent cause of death?